Piano • Vocal • Guitar

CRAIG CARNELIA
SONGBOOK

EXPANDED EDITION

All Piano Arrangements by Craig Carnelia
except for those songs written with and arranged by Marvin Hamlisch.

ISBN-13: 978-0-7935-2816-5
ISBN-10: 0-7935-2816-X

HAL•LEONARD®
CORPORATION
7777 W. BLUEMOUND RD. P.O. BOX 13819 MILWAUKEE, WI 53213

In Australia Contact:
Hal Leonard Australia Pty. Ltd.
4 Lentara Court • Cheltenham, Victoria, 3192 Australia • Email: ausadmin@halleonard.com

For all works contained herein:
Unauthorized copying, arranging, adapting, recording or public performance is an infringement of copyright.
Infringers are liable under the law.

Visit Hal Leonard Online at
www.halleonard.com

BIOGRAPHY

Performing "Flight" at the Eugene O'Neill Theatre Center.
Photo: A. Vincent Scarano

Craig Carnelia places in the rarified group acclaimed as a songwriters' songwriter… *Wall Street Journal* reporter, Roxane Orgill, wrote "Craig Carnelia's songs wrap you up and carry you off, just like the old songs did — those by Irving Berlin, Richard Rodgers, Lorenz Hart, Jerome Kern, Cole Porter and the Gershwins. And yet his songs are modern in their lyrics, rhythm and harmony." Sheldon Harnick, lyricist of FIDDLER ON THE ROOF, SHE LOVES ME and others, referred more personally when he said that "Carnelia has a unique musical voice. His uniqueness comes from making a synthesis between theater music and certain elements of rock, so that the music sounds contemporary and traditional at the same time."

Craig Brian Carnelia was born in Floral Park, New York, on August 13, 1949. He began writing songs at the age of 15 and around the same time, became a frequent theatergoer, thanks to his older brother James. In 1969, Craig moved to Manhattan and worked professionally as an actor for a short time, including a six-month run as The Boy in THE FANTASTICKS, Off-Broadway, before turning his attention full-time to writing.

The cabaret renaissance in the mid '70s offered Craig frequent opportunities to appear at the legendary downtown club Reno Sweeney, playing and singing from his own expanding catalogue of songs, as an opening act for such diverse talents as Diane Keaton, Warhol superstar Holly Woodlawn and Andrea Marcovicci. Also down at Reno's, he met Karen Akers, who along with Marcovicci has been performing his songs ever since. Others on the long and eclectic list of singers who have performed and recorded his songs are Barbara Cook, John Lithgow, Barry Manilow, Karen Mason, Julie Wilson, Amanda McBroom, Betty Buckley, Jason Alexander, Sally Mayes, Tovah Feldshuh, Sam Harris, Ellen Greene, Raoul Esparza, Sutton Foster, Sharon McNight, Judy Kuhn, Marin Mazie, Lisa Asher and Eric Michael Gillett, who recorded an entire CD of Carnelia songs entitled CAST OF THOUSANDS.

Carnelia's career as a theater composer began in 1977 when Stephen Schwartz asked him to join the team of songwriters he was putting together for an upcoming musical he was directing based on Studs Terkel's book WORKING. The team was to include James Taylor, Micki Grant, Mary Rodgers & Susan Birkenhead, and Schwartz himself. Craig contributed 4 songs to the show, 2 of which, "The Mason" and "Just A Housewife," are found in this songbook. WORKING opened at the 46th Street Theatre (now the Richard Rodgers) on May 14, 1978 and earned this exceptional writer his first Tony® Award nomination. The cast album was recorded on Columbia Records and later reissued on CD by Sony Music.

During the writing of WORKING Craig read the popular non-fiction book IS THERE LIFE AFTER HIGH SCHOOL? by Ralph Keyes. As soon as WORKING opened he set to work on a musical version of the book with playwright Jeffrey Kindley. IS THERE LIFE AFTER HIGH SCHOOL? opened at the Ethel Barrymore Theatre on May 3, 1982 and featured Carnelia's first full score for Broadway. The cast album was released on Original Cast Records. HIGH SCHOOL is represented here by three songs: "The Kid Inside," "Things I Learned In High School" and "Nothing Really Happened." One of these, "The Kid Inside," was given wide exposure by Barry Manilow when he included it on his "Showstoppers" album, along with another of Craig's songs, "You Can Have The TV."

In 1987, Craig wrote the music and lyrics for the Off-Broadway musical 3 POSTCARDS, presented at Playwrights Horizons. Small and eccentric, the show was written with Craig Lucas and is in every way an "original." It was named one of the year's 10-Best in TIME Magazine, is included in the Burns-Mantle anthology BEST PLAYS OF 1986-1987 as Best Musical of the Season and was successfully revived in 1994 by Circle Rep. One of Carnelia's most frequently performed songs, the haunting "Picture In The Hall" was first heard in 3 POSTCARDS. Also Off-Broadway, he contributed single songs to THE NO-FRILLS REVUE, DIAMONDS and A...MY NAME IS STILL ALICE. DIAMONDS was directed by Hal Prince at the Circle In The Square Downtown and included Carnelia's classic baseball song "What You'd Call A Dream," also found in this collection.

The 1990s began with a great success in a tiny venue when a revue of the composer's work entitled PICTURES IN THE HALL opened at Eighty Eight's, a popular club in Greenwich Village. The show earned Carnelia a Bistro Award and 3 MAC Awards (given by the Manhattan Association of Cabarets & Clubs) and brought him to even greater prominence as one of his generation's finest songwriters. Other honors in this period included the Kleban Award for distinguished lyric writing, the first annual Gilman & Gonzalez-Falla Musical Theatre Award, the Johnny Mercer Award as "Emerging American Songwriter" and a fourth MAC Award as Songwriter of the Year, for his song "Flight."

In 1997, producer Marty Bell was gathering talent to write a musical based on the classic film SWEET SMELL OF SUCCESS. The book was being written by John Guare, Marvin Hamlisch had been chosen to compose the music and they were looking for the right lyricist. Hamlisch & Carnelia met, liked each other, wrote four songs to see what these two dissimilar talents might be like as a team and were immediately signed to collaborate on the score. Soon thereafter, Nicholas Hytner was brought in to direct. After the whole group met at Hamlisch's apartment for the first time and Hytner, Guare and Bell had gone home, Craig and Marvin stood in the kitchen, drinking a toast to their show, vowing to "enjoy the ride." And enjoy it they did. SWEET SMELL OF SUCCESS opened on March 14, 2002 at the Martin Beck Theatre (now the Hirschfeld), starring John Lithgow and Brian d'Arcy James. Hamlisch and Carnelia received both Drama Desk and Tony® Award nominations for their score. Together they also co-produced the critically acclaimed cast album for Sony Music. Three songs from the show are represented in this volume.

While working on SWEET SMELL, Hamlisch and Carnelia were asked to write the songs for Nora Ephron's play with music, IMAGINARY FRIENDS. The play concerned the legendary feud between Lillian Hellman and Mary McCarthy, with songs serving primarily as commentary and contrast to the action. IMAGINARY FRIENDS opened on December 12, 2002 at the Ethel Barrymore Theatre. It was directed by Jack O'Brien and starred Cherry Jones and Swoosie Kurtz as the two warring writers. Craig received his second Drama Desk nomination for his versatile and literate lyrics. Included here is the title song from the show, as well as "Smart Women" and "Words Fail Me," two songs that were created for but not included in the Broadway production.

Ironically, these two cut songs are among Craig's favorite pieces he has ever written with composer Marvin Hamlisch.

You will discover two songs in this book from another recent original musical entitled ACTOR, LAWYER, INDIAN CHIEF. The show was written with playwright-director David H. Bell and has been produced around the country, most notably by Goodspeed Musicals at their Norma Terris Theatre. "The Man In 37A" and "Cowboy Waltz" are but a taste of what Carnelia considers his finest score to date. Also with David H. Bell, Craig has co-authored THE GOOD WAR, a musical based on Studs Terkel's Pulitzer Prize winning book on World War II. Using Terkel's text and unique, new arrangements of vintage songs of the '40s, the show was commissioned by Northlight Theatre in Chicago and had its World Premiere in 2004, making Carnelia the only writer with two Studs Terkel musicals to his credit.

In 1992, Craig began a second career, as a teacher, and has come to prize this work as deeply as his writing. For the past fourteen years he has been teaching his own musical theater acting classes professionally in New York. At present he teaches twenty hours a week in the city and often travels to universities around the country to hold master classes. He also serves as a mentor to young writers in various workshops and programs throughout the country.

Craig is a longtime member of both ASCAP and The Dramatists Guild and has served on the Guild's council since 1995.

October, 2006

In a tribute to Johnny Mercer
hosted by Michael Feinstein at the
Weill Recital Hall at Carnegie Hall.

At Right Track Recording Studios the day the original cast album of SWEET SMELL OF SUCCESS was recorded. Left to right: Marvin Hamlisch, Brian d'Arcy James, John Guare, Carnelia and John Lithgow.

Photo: Chris Ottaunick

At 890 Studios with collaborator Marvin Hamlisch during rehearsals for SWEET SMELL OF SUCCESS.

Photo: Peter Roth

Under the marquee with the brilliant Cherry Jones, one of the stars of Hamlisch and Carnelia's second collaboration, IMAGINARY FRIENDS.

Photo: Michael Ian

At pre-opening celebration for WICKED, with WORKING collaborator and friend of many years, Stephen Schwartz.

Photo: R.J. Capak

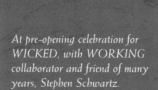

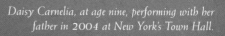

Daisy Carnelia, at age nine, performing with her father in 2004 at New York's Town Hall.

Photo: Maryann Lopinto

Opening night of Barry Manilow's *"Showstoppers Revue"* at the Paramount Theatre. Pictured here with Manilow and legendary songwriters Sammy Cahn, Jule Styne, Burton Lane and Cy Coleman.

Photo: R.J. Capak

Enjoying a break while rehearsing with Broadway and cabaret star Karen Akers

Photo: Michael Ian

Talking with Liza Minnelli after giving a solo concert at the Russian Tea Room.

Photo: R.J. Capak

Rehearsing a new song in the quiet of the afternoon at the Oak Room of the Algonquin Hotel with Andrea Marcovicci.

Photo: Michael Ian

With dear friend and Broadway great, Burton Lane (FINIAN'S RAINBOW, ON A CLEAR DAY…) at the American Society of Composers, Authors and Publishers (ASCAP), upon winning the Kleban Award.

Photo: R.J. Capak

*Backstage at the International Festival of the Arts,
having just had the pleasure of sharing the stage
with the great Rosemary Clooney.*

Photo: R.J. Capak

With Lisa Brescia at opening night party for
SWEET SMELL OF SUCCESS.

*Studs Terkel being Studs Terkel, with
collaborators David H. Bell and Carnelia
during the World Premiere production of
THE GOOD WAR at Northlight Theatre
in Chicago.*

Photo: Michael Brosilow

*Backstage at the 92nd Street "Y," sharing the
"Lyrics & Lyricists" bill with Lynn Ahrens,
Stephen Flaherty and David Zippel.*

*Left to right: (front row)
Carnelia, Lynn Ahrens, Lucie Arnaz,
Stephen Flaherty,
(back row)
Marilyn and Alan Bergman,
ASCAP's Michael Kerker, David Zippel.*

Photo: R.J. Capak

FLIGHT

Music and Lyric by
CRAIG CARNELIA

Copyright © 1992 Big A Music LLC
Administered by A. Schroeder International LLC
200 West 51st Street, Suite 1009, New York, New York 10019
International Copyright Secured   All Rights Reserved

(*) - Play both the written note and the note an octave lower.

* "Ay" sound flows directly from "Ah" sound and is pronounced "Ay" as in "way".

THE MASON

from the Broadway Musical WORKING

Music and Lyric by
CRAIG CARNELIA

Copyright © 1978 Big A Music LLC
Administered by A. Schroeder International LLC
200 West 51st Street, Suite 1009, New York, New York 10019
International Copyright Secured   All Rights Reserved

JUST A HOUSEWIFE

from the Broadway Musical WORKING

Music and Lyric by
CRAIG CARNELIA

Copyright © 1978 Big A Music LLC
Administered by A. Schroeder International LLC
200 West 51st Street, Suite 1009, New York, New York 10019
International Copyright Secured   All Rights Reserved

*alternate lyric

THE KID INSIDE
from the Broadway Musical IS THERE LIFE AFTER HIGH SCHOOL?

Music and Lyric by
CRAIG CARNELIA

Copyright © 1983 Big A Music LLC
Administered by A. Schroeder International LLC
200 West 51st Street, Suite 1009, New York, New York 10019
International Copyright Secured   All Rights Reserved

THINGS I LEARNED IN HIGH SCHOOL

from the Broadway Musical IS THERE LIFE AFTER HIGH SCHOOL?

Music and Lyric by
CRAIG CARNELIA

Copyright © 1983 Big A Music LLC
Administered by A. Schroeder International LLC
200 West 51st Street, Suite 1009, New York, New York 10019
International Copyright Secured All Rights Reserved

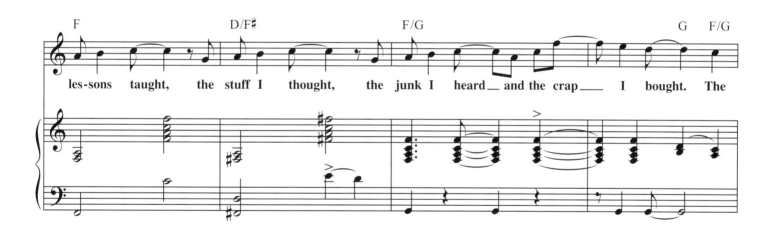

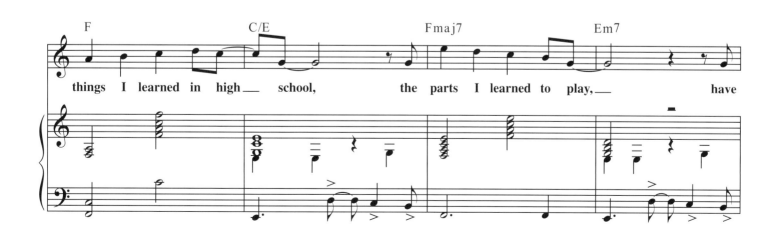

hopes I held ___ and the fears ___ I fought. The things I learned in high ___ school ___ have

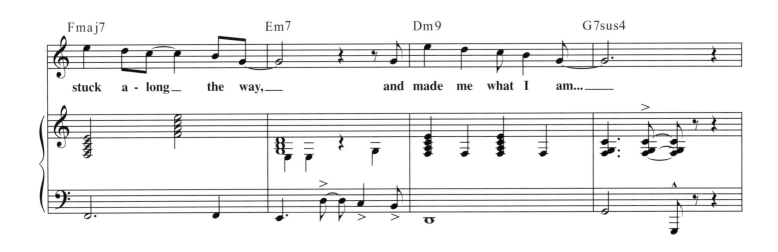

stuck a - long ___ the way, ___ and made me what I am... ___

Thanks a lot. Thanks ___ a lot for all the les - sons I learned.

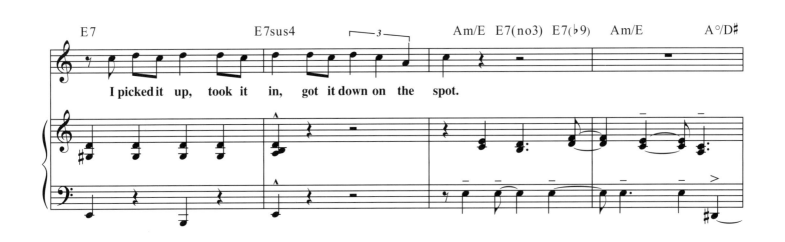

I picked it up, took it in, got it down on the spot.

Thanks a lot. Thanks___ a lot to all the par - ties con - cerned,_____ for the

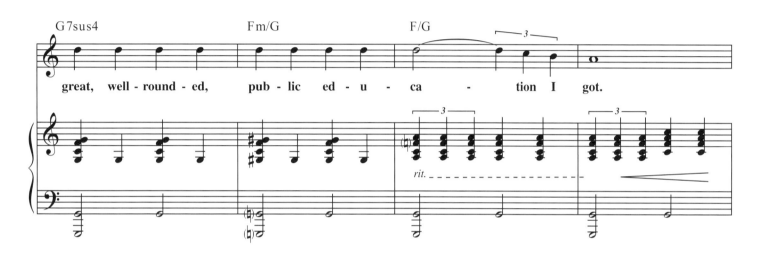

great, well - round - ed, pub - lic ed - u - ca - tion I got.

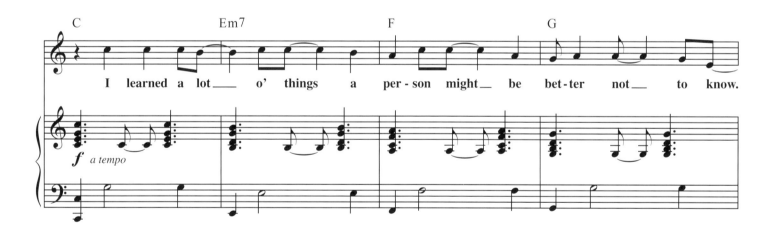

I learned a lot___ o' things a per - son might___ be bet - ter not___ to know.

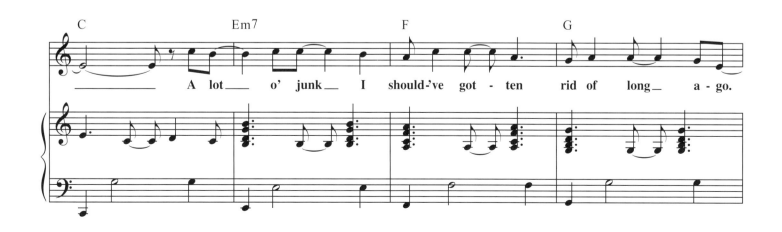

_____ A lot___ o' junk___ I should've got - ten rid of long___ a - go.

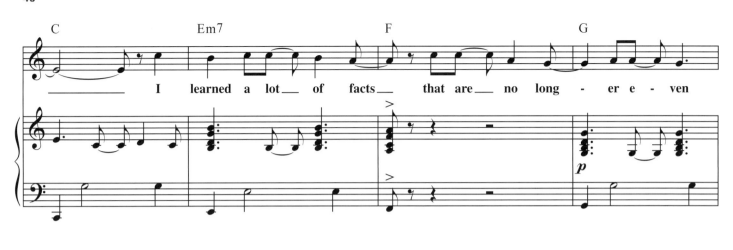

I learned a lot __ of facts __ that are __ no long - er e - ven

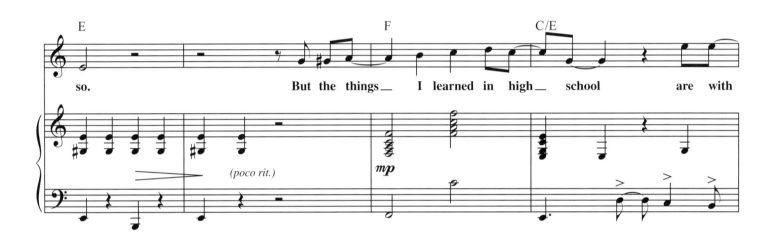

so. But the things __ I learned in high __ school are with

(poco rit.)

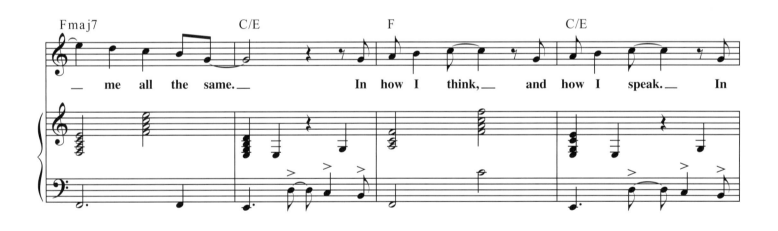

__ me all the same. __ In how I think, __ and how I speak. __ In

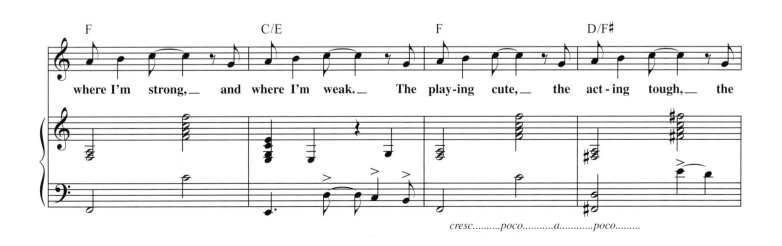

where I'm strong, __ and where I'm weak. The play-ing cute, __ the act-ing tough, __ the

cresc..........poco...........a............poco........

NOTHING REALLY HAPPENED

from the Broadway Musical IS THERE LIFE AFTER HIGH SCHOOL?

Music and Lyric by
CRAIG CARNELIA

Copyright © 1983 Big A Music LLC
Administered by A. Schroeder International LLC
200 West 51st Street, Suite 1009, New York, New York 10019
International Copyright Secured   All Rights Reserved

COME ON, SNOW

Music and Lyric by
CRAIG CARNELIA

Bright, Hoedown feel (♩ = 122)

Come on snow, come down,__ come on__ and make__ it quick.__

Come on snow, come down,__ come on__ and make__ it stick.__

Come on snow, don't lose your cool,__ 'cause I don't wan-na go__ to school.

Copyright © 1993 Big A Music LLC
Administered by A. Schroeder International LLC
200 West 51st Street, Suite 1009, New York, New York 10019
International Copyright Secured   All Rights Reserved

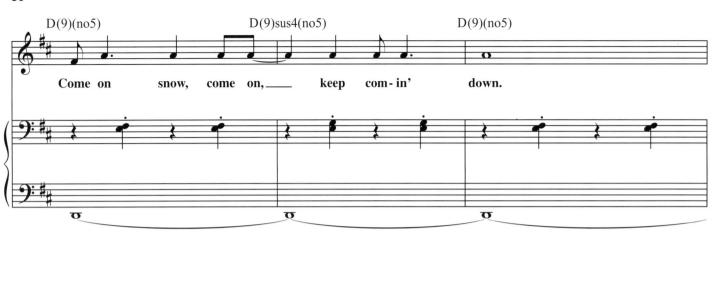

Come on snow, come on,___ keep com-in' down.

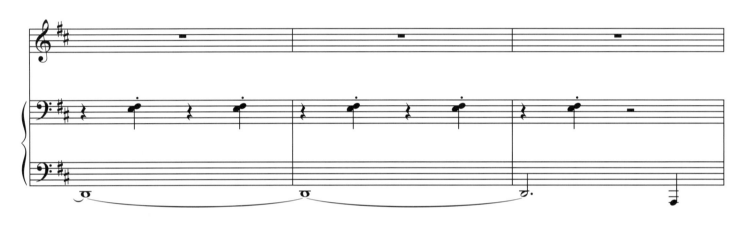

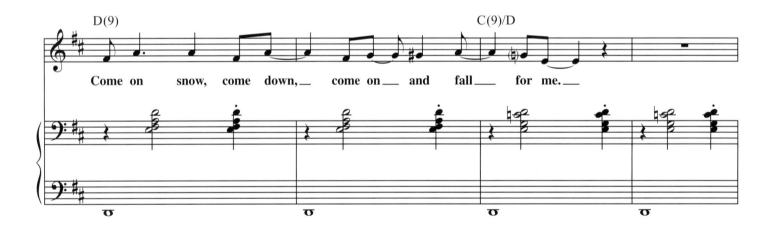

Come on snow, come down,__ come on__ and fall___ for me.__

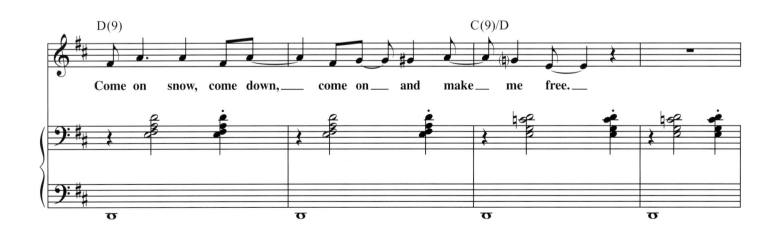

Come on snow, come down,___ come on__ and make__ me free.__

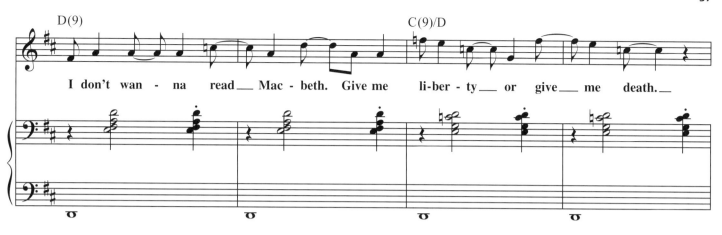

I don't wan - na read__ Mac - beth. Give me li - ber - ty__ or give__ me death.__

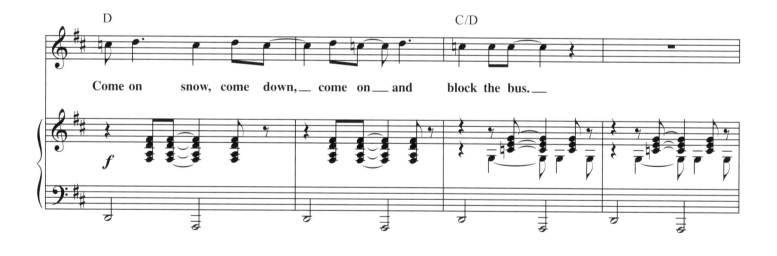

Come on snow, come on,__ keep com - in' down.

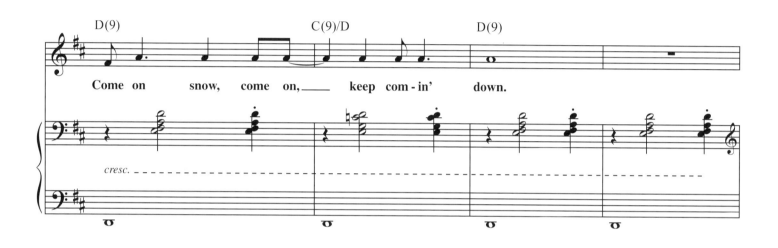

Come on snow, come down,__ come on__ and block the bus.__

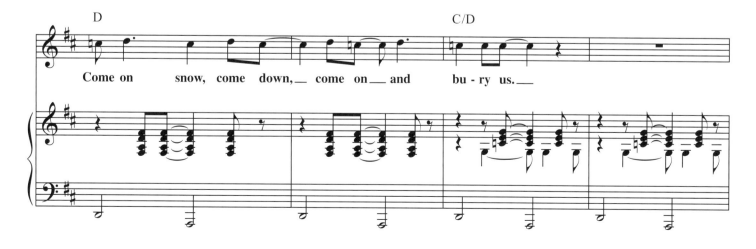

Come on snow, come down,__ come on__ and bu - ry us.__

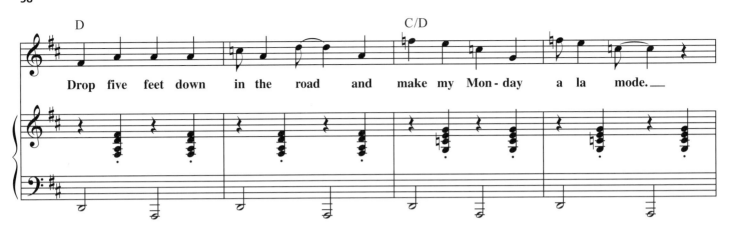

Drop five feet down in the road and make my Mon-day a la mode.

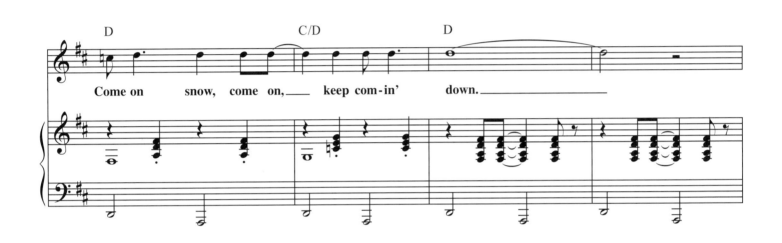

Come on snow, come on,___ keep com-in' down.___

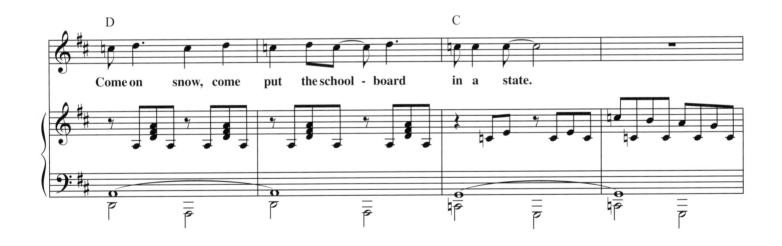

Come on snow, come put the school - board in a state.

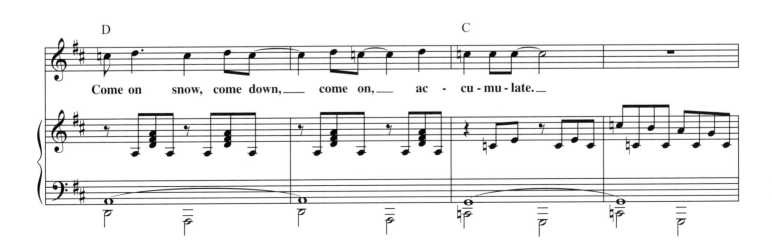

Come on snow, come down,___ come on,___ ac - cu - mu - late.___

* - Alternate Lyric

MAGELLAN

Music and Lyric by
CRAIG CARNELIA

Copyright © 1993 Big A Music LLC
Administered A. Schroeder International LLC
200 West 51st Street, Suite 1009, New York, New York 10019
International Copyright Secured   All Rights Reserved

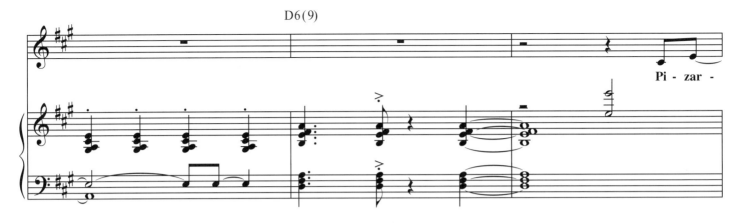

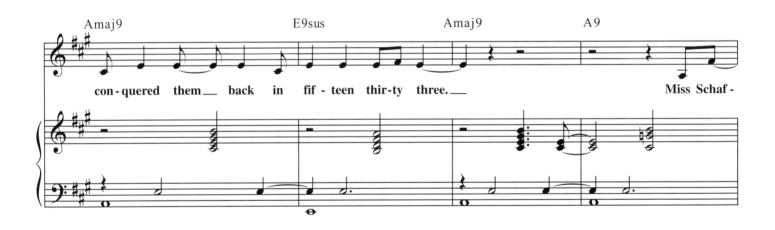

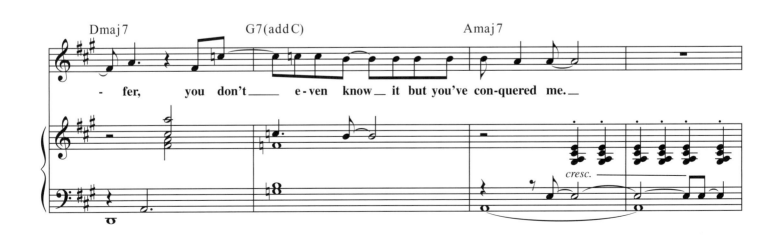

Harder 2

The names and dates will not be with me in a year or two.

Breezy 2

But I'll al-ways re-mem-ber you.

I'll al-ways re-mem-ber you. I'll al-

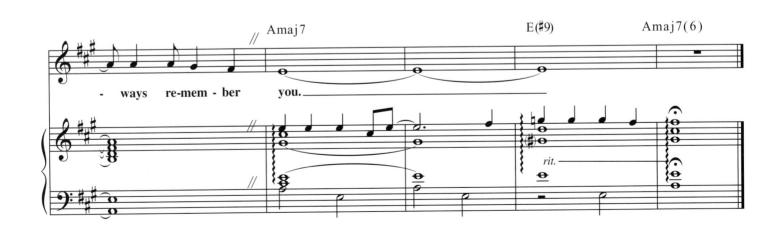

-ways re-mem-ber you.

LIFE ON EARTH

Music and Lyric by
CRAIG CARNELIA

(*) - *Play both the written note and the note an octave lower.*

Copyright © 1991 Big A Music LLC
Administered by A. Schroeder International LLC
200 West 51st Street, Suite 1009, New York, New York 10019
International Copyright Secured   All Rights Reserved

WHAT YOU'D CALL A DREAM

from the Off-Broadway Revue DIAMONDS

Music and Lyric by
CRAIG CARNELIA

Copyright © 1991 Big A Music LLC
Administered by A. Schroeder International LLC
200 West 51st Street, Suite 1009, New York, New York 10019
International Copyright Secured   All Rights Reserved

THE PICTURE IN THE HALL

from the Musical Play 3 POSTCARDS

Music and Lyric by
CRAIG CARNELIA

In her hand ___ she holds a small bou - quet. ___

In the dis - tance there's a Chev - ro - let. ___

In the cor - ner there's a tree, ___ on - ly half _

Copyright © 1991 Big A Music LLC
Administered by A. Schroeder International LLC
200 West 51st Street, Suite 1009, New York, New York 10019
International Copyright Secured   All Rights Reserved

LOOK IN MY EYES

Music and Lyric by
CRAIG CARNELIA

Copyright © 1992 Big A Music LLC
Administered by A. Schroeder International LLC
200 West 51st Street, Suite 1009, New York, New York 10019
International Copyright Secured   All Rights Reserved

I MET A MAN TODAY

Music and Lyric by
CRAIG CARNELIA

Copyright © 1973 Big A Music LLC
Copyright Renewed
Administered by A. Schroeder International LLC
200 West 51st Street, Suite 1009, New York, New York 10019
International Copyright Secured   All Rights Reserved

YOU CAN HAVE THE T.V.

Music and Lyric by
CRAIG CARNELIA

Copyright © 1972, 1991 Big A Music LLC
Copyright Renewed
Administered by A. Schroeder International LLC
200 West 51st Street, Suite 1009, New York, New York 10019
International Copyright Secured   All Rights Reserved

*alternate lyric

ONE TRACK MIND

from the Broadway Musical SWEET SMELL OF SUCCESS

Music by MARVIN HAMLISCH
Lyric by CRAIG CARNELIA

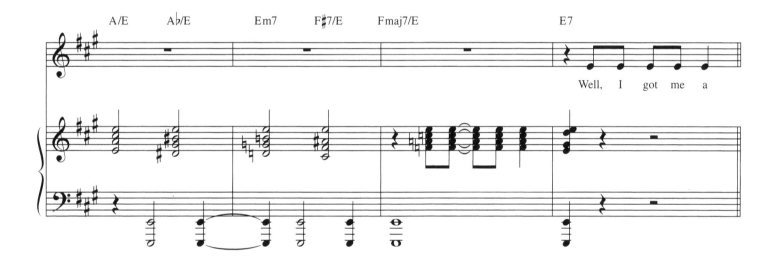

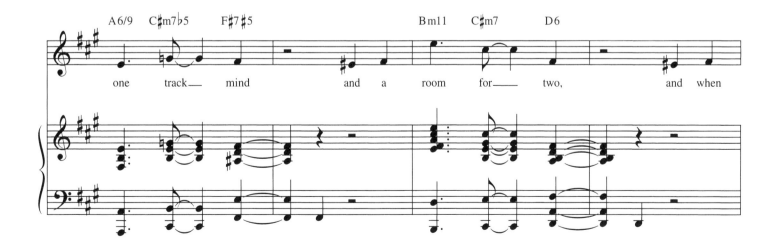

Copyright © 2002 by Red Bullet Music and Big A Music LLC
All Rights for Red Bullet Music Administered by Famous Music Corporation
All Rights for Big A Music LLC Administered by A. Schroeder International LLC, 200 West 51st Street, Suite 1009, New York, NY 10019
International Copyright Secured   All Rights Reserved

AT THE FOUNTAIN
(Reprise)
from the Broadway Musical SWEET SMELL OF SUCCESS

Music by MARVIN HAMLISCH
Lyric by CRAIG CARNELIA

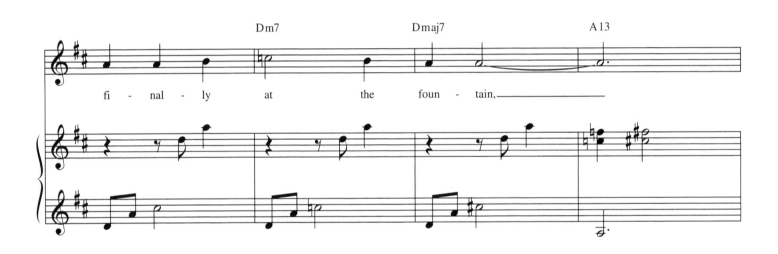

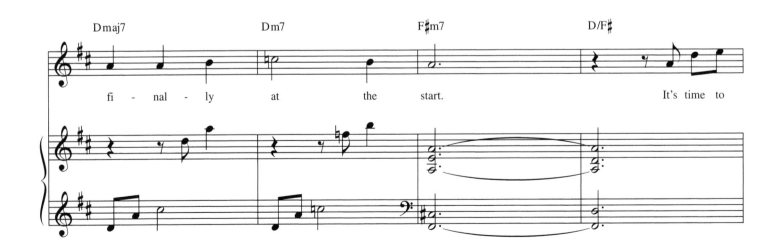

Copyright © 2002 by Red Bullet Music and Big A Music LLC
All Rights for Red Bullet Music Administered by Famous Music Corporation
All Rights for Big A Music LLC Administered by A. Schroeder International LLC, 200 West 51st Street, Suite 1009, New York, NY 10019
International Copyright Secured   All Rights Reserved

I CANNOT HEAR THE CITY

from the Broadway Musical SWEET SMELL OF SUCCESS

Music by MARVIN HAMLISCH
Lyric by CRAIG CARNELIA

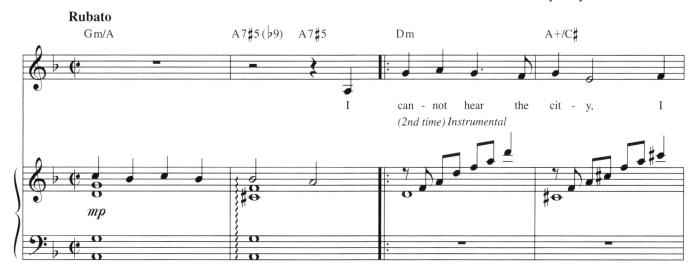

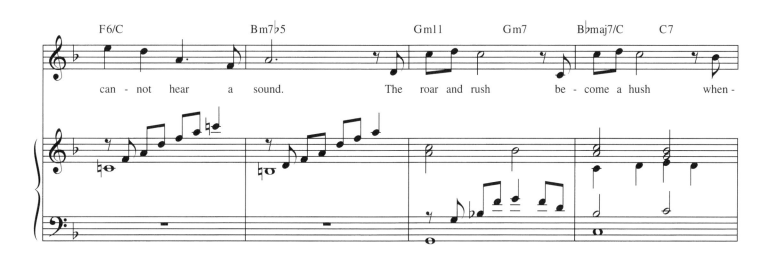

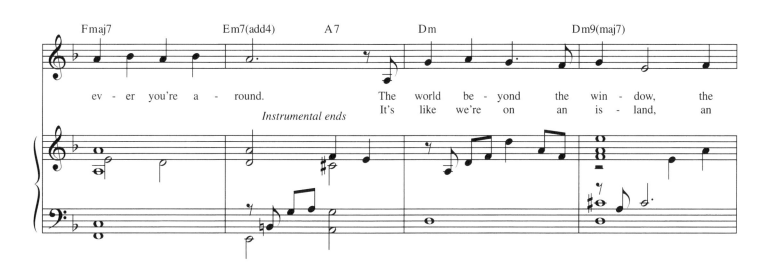

Copyright © 2002 by Red Bullet Music and Big A Music LLC
All Rights for Red Bullet Music Administered by Famous Music Corporation
All Rights for Big A Music LLC Administered by A. Schroeder International LLC, 200 West 51st Street, Suite 1009, New York, NY 10019
International Copyright Secured   All Rights Reserved

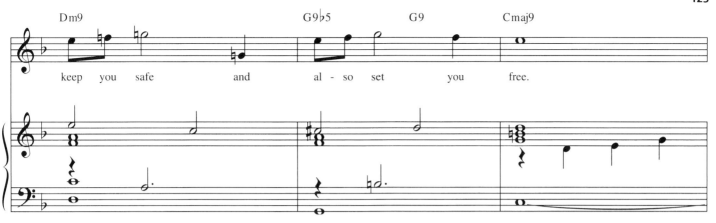

keep you safe and al - so set you free.

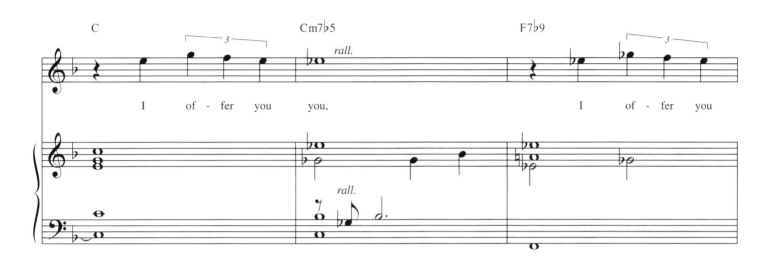

I of - fer you you, I of - fer you

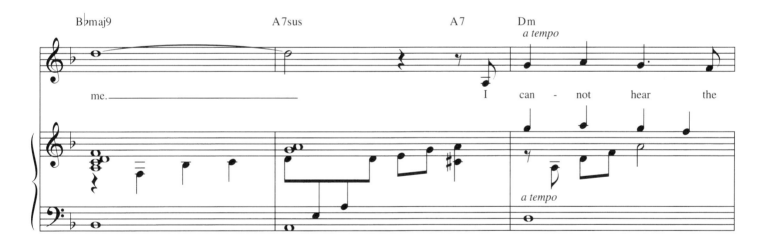

me. I can - not hear the

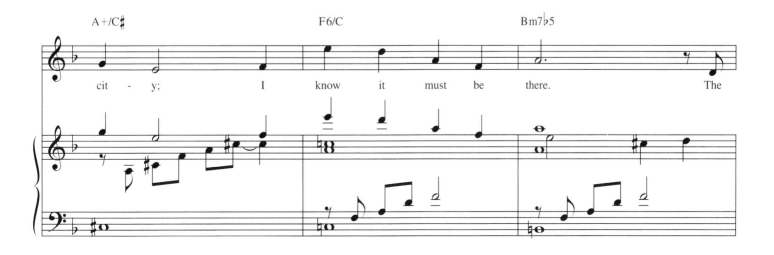

cit - y; I know it must be there. The

COWBOY WALTZ

from the Musical ACTOR, LAWYER, INDIAN CHIEF

Music and Lyric by
CRAIG CARNELIA

Moderate Folk Waltz (♩ = 154)

Note: gently accent downbeats throughout song.

Copyright © 1995 Big A Music LLC
Administered by A. Schroeder International LLC
200 West 51st Street, Suite 1009, New York, New York 10019
International Copyright Secured   All Rights Reserved

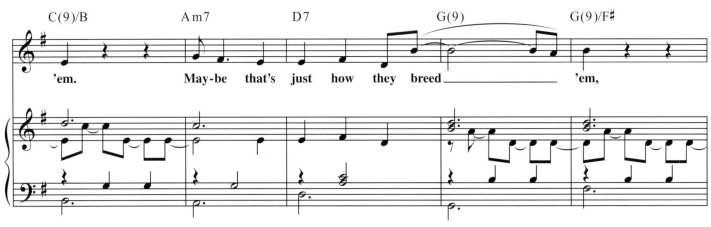

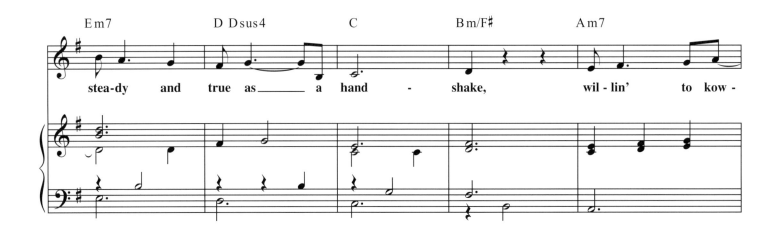

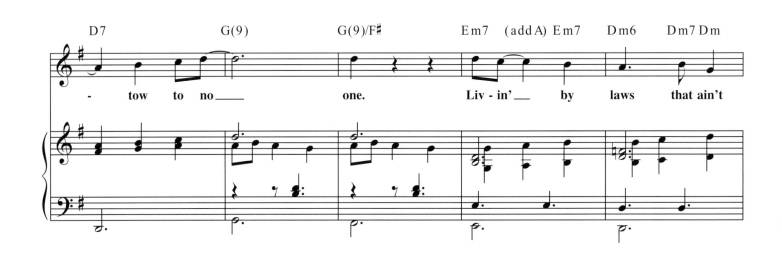

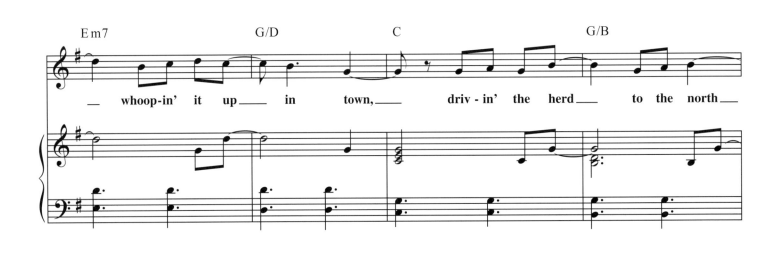

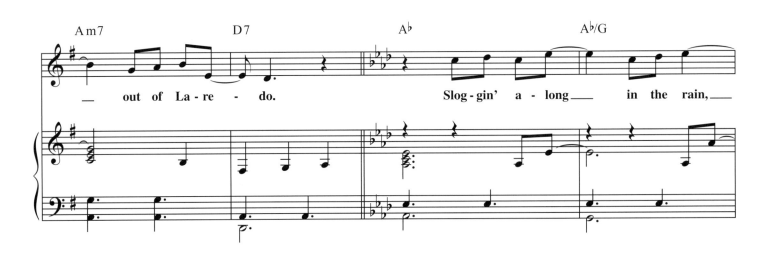

THE MAN IN 37A

from the Musical ACTOR, LAWYER, INDIAN CHIEF

Music and Lyric by
CRAIG CARNELIA

Copyright © 1996 Big A Music LLC
Administered by A. Schroeder International LLC
200 West 51st Street, Suite 1009, New York, New York 10019
International Copyright Secured   All Rights Reserved

136

Tin-ker, tai-lor, ac - ro-bat, clown, sol-dier, farm-er, man____ a-bout town, the
Ban-ker, ba-ker, bus - 'ness ty-coon, cow-boy, king, the man____ in the moon, the

man in thir - ty-se-ven A?____ No way.____
man in thir - ty-se-ven A?____ No way.____

(2nd time only) Hit me a-gain.____

He turns off the light and tears____ through the night, like oth -

What do you wan-na be when you grow up? — Doc - tor, Law - yer, In -

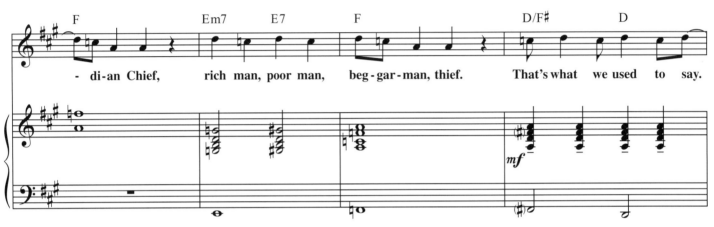

- di-an Chief, rich man, poor man, beg - gar-man, thief. That's what we used to say.

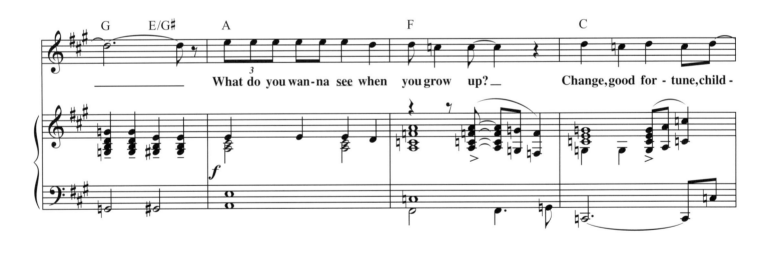

What do you wan-na see when you grow up? — Change, good for - tune, child -

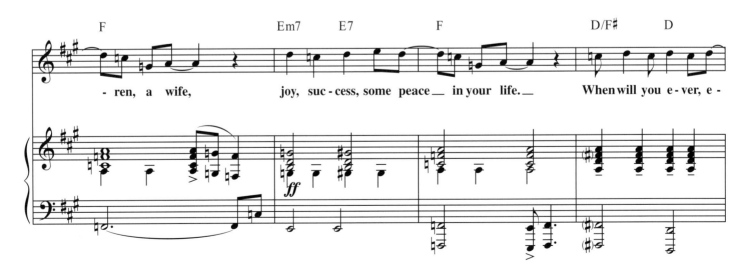

- ren, a wife, joy, suc - cess, some peace — in your life. — When will you e - ver, e -

IMAGINARY FRIEND
from the Play With Music IMAGINARY FRIENDS

Music by MARVIN HAMLISCH
Lyric by CRAIG CARNELIA

Copyright © 2002 by Red Bullet Music and Big A Music LLC
All Rights for Red Bullet Music Administered by Famous Music Corporation
All Rights for Big A Music LLC Administered by A. Schroeder International LLC, 200 West 51st Street, Suite 1009, New York, NY 10019
International Copyright Secured   All Rights Reserved

SMART WOMEN

written for the Play With Music IMAGINARY FRIENDS

Music by MARVIN HAMLISCH
Lyric by CRAIG CARNELIA

Copyright © 2002 by Red Bullet Music and Big A Music LLC
All Rights for Red Bullet Music Administered by Famous Music Corporation
All Rights for Big A Music LLC Administered by A. Schroeder International LLC, 200 West 51st Street, Suite 1009, New York, NY 10019
International Copyright Secured   All Rights Reserved

WORDS FAIL ME

written for the Play With Music IMAGINARY FRIENDS

Music by MARVIN HAMLISCH
Lyric by CRAIG CARNELIA

Copyright © 2002 by Red Bullet Music and Big A Music LLC
All Rights for Red Bullet Music Administered by Famous Music Corporation
All Rights for Big A Music LLC Administered by A. Schroeder International LLC, 200 West 51st Street, Suite 1009, New York, NY 10019
International Copyright Secured   All Rights Reserved

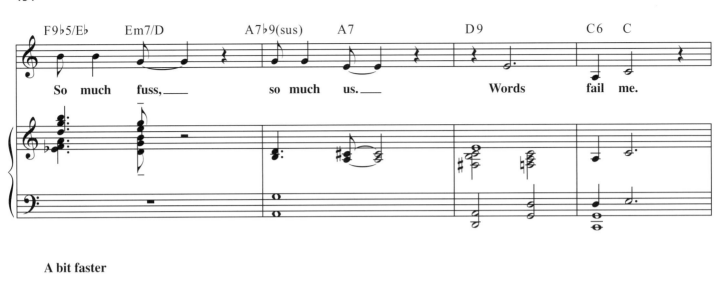

A bit faster

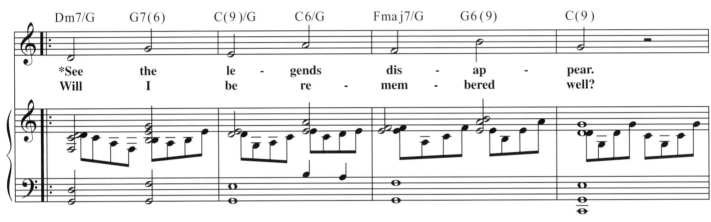

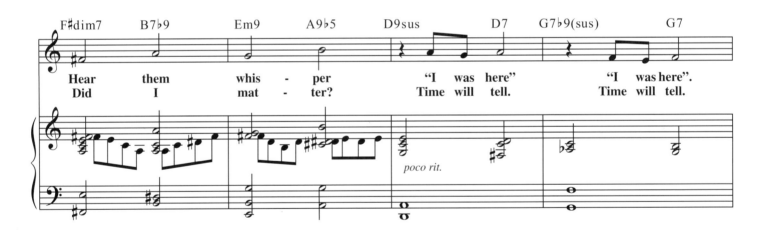

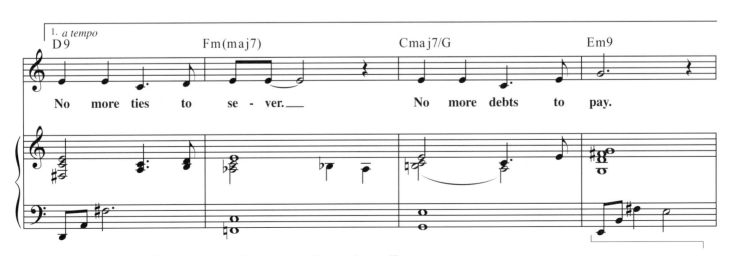

* (Alternate Lyric - "One by one we disappear, with a whisper...")

LOOK FOR ME IN THE SONGS

Music and Lyric by
CRAIG CARNELIA

Copyright © 2000 Big A Music LLC
Administered by A. Schroeder International LLC
200 West 51st Street, Suite 1009, New York, New York 10019
International Copyright Secured   All Rights Reserved

* (Alternate Female Lyric)